A Christian Response to Relativism:

Jihadism's Best Friend

By
John Ruiz M. Div., BCC

A Christian Response to Relativism:
Jihadism's Best Friend

Copyright © 2021 by *John Ruiz M. Div., BCC*

ISBN
978-1-954932-34-0 (Paperback)
978-1-954932-33-3 (eBook)

To Kristy
whose love and encouragement
gave me the courage to write this book.

Contents

A Christian Response to Relativism:
Jihadism' Best Friend

I came that they may have life,
and have it abundantly.
John 10:10b

To begin a discussion on relativism, jihadism and a Christian response of good news and hope; it is imperative to define what each is and what are some of the main characteristics that distinguish each of these worldviews.

Let us begin with a Christian worldview looking at God, neighbor, sin and the role of the church. To summarize a Christian understanding of God let us turn to the 15th century Christian thinker St. John of the Cross who understood God's activity in the world this way:

> Since God is wise, he loves you with
> wisdom.
> Since God is good, he loves you with
> goodness.
> Since God is holy, he loves you with
> holiness.
> Since God is just, he loves you with
> justice.
> Since God is merciful, he loves you with
> mercy.
> Since God is compassionate and
> understanding

he loves you with gentleness and
sweetness. [1]

The parable of the Good Samaritan taught by Jesus *(Luke 10:25-37)* challenges us with the idea that *everyone* is my neighbor. Therefore, if everyone is my neighbor then everyone is to be treated with dignity, respect and love. For, *God is love (I John 4:8b)*. And, love in action is the call for all believers. *The commandment we have from him is this: those who love God must love their brothers and sisters also (I John 4:21).*

Further, one's human value does not come from what one does but rather one's value comes from one's being. God gives life and from this gift lies intrinsic value in each human life. *In the beginning was the Word, and the Word was with God, and the Word was God. He was in the beginning with God. All things came into being through him and without him not one thing came into being. What has come into being in him was life, and the life was the light of all people. The light shines in the darkness, and the darkness did not overcome it (John 1:1-5).*

St. John of the Cross wrote from this point of view when he penned these words, "When our hearts are free from liking and judging people merely according to their natural gifts, we are not held captive by external and changing charms. We are instead free to love people as they really are, and we can penetrate more easily to their core personality, their true goodness." [2]

A concept of sin within a Christian worldview can be seen in many different ways. For the purpose of this

1   Sister Elizabeth Ruth ODC, *Daily Readings with St. John of the Cross* (Templegate Publishers: Springfield, Illinois) 1985, p. 46.

2   Ibid, p. 40.

discussion John Wesley the founder of the Wesleyan/ Methodist movement is a good starting point. For Wesley sin is not a thing rather, "Wesley spoke of sin on relational terms. His classic definition is that sin is 'every voluntary breach of the law of love'. At its base, sin is a broken relationship, whether that brokenness is expressed toward others or toward God. And it is important to note that breach is conscious and willful." [3]

The effects of sin are universal and since sin is not a thing that one can conquer or extinguish through human effort then there is the necessity for something outside of us to restore the right relationship of intimacy with God and man. This occurs through the life, death and resurrection of Jesus. "For, you see, we need a Savior only if we need saving; we need a Savior only if we cannot save ourselves. This is precisely what Wesley, in his doctrine of sin, calls us to acknowledge." [4]

The role of the church is to represent the good news of Jesus Christ to the world through word and deed. Jesus taught a parable instructing believers where he said, *"for I was hungry and you gave me food, I was thirsty and you gave me something to drink, I was a stranger and you welcomed me, I was naked and you gave me clothing, I was sick and you took care of me, I was in prison and you visited me (Matthew 25;35-36).*

Francis Cardinal Arinze in his book, *Religions for Peace: A Call for Solidarity to the Religions of the World,* wrote these words concerning the role of the church and religions of the world. "Human life is sacred. It must be protected. We have no right to kill ourselves or to kill innocent people.

---

3   Steve Harper, The Way to Heaven: The Gospel According to John Wesley (Zondervan: Grand Rapids, Michigan) 2003, p. 23.

4   Ibid.

While self-defense is a right and justifiable, it has to be kept within due limits. Justice, peace, tranquility in the world are built on the pillars of respect for the fundamental rights of other people, especially their right to life, religious freedom, and free exercise of political, economic, and cultural rights. Economic and political development of peoples is also an obligatory road to peace. If people are illiterate, underdeveloped, oppressed and repressed, then justice and peace are rendered more difficult. Violence, terrorism, the taking of human lives and the destruction of property are condemned by all genuine religions. They are opposed to love of God and neighbor. No matter the problems and challenges to be faced, these violent roads are the wrong ones. Solutions in line with respect for God and humanity have to be sought, no matter how difficult and long-term they may be. All religions are bound to help their followers to engage in reflections such as these." [5]

Relativism is a worldview that attempts to uphold individual liberties, individual thought and individual freedoms as foundational for self-fulfillment and societal progress. On face value it is a worldview that can be very seductive. Live for today! A popular song from the recent past sang, "If you can't be with the one you love then love the one, you're with".

Many times, though not all, notions of God are discarded. Followed by the rejection of any discernible knowledge of any absolute truth. Instead, truth is in the eye of the beholder.

Oddly, relativism struggles with treating those outside their worldview in the same way as they would like to be

---

5   Francis Cardinal Marine, *Religions for Peace: A Call for Solidarity to the Religions of the World* (Doubleday a division of Random House, Inc.: NewYork, New York) 2002, p. vii.

treated. This is especially true for those persons within one's community who do hold and live by absolute truths.

Sin is rejected since there is no uniform standard to define the parameters of sin. And in many cases since there is no longer a need for a Savior the concept of Jesus, who is the Savior of the world, becomes a thing of the past. Jesus becomes a pleasant myth and salvation is no longer needed by modern man.

Finally, the role of the church, for those who maintain a desire for the church, becomes a type of social club gathering of like-minded people who may, at times, band together for a cause that unites them. Religion becomes a collection of nice and sometimes helpful ideas that can be good for you. Like going to the gym or regular doctor's appointments or improving. one's diet.

One of the problems, however, of relativism is meaning in life. If anything goes then does anything really matter? A worldview that insists, "It's okay to do this or that as long as I'm not hurting anybody" seems to forget that no one is an island. We all live in social communities with other people. Therefore, individual acts always, in some way, impact other people. Those around us. Those who care for and love us.

Finally, since relativism has no consistent foundation to discern between good and evil it also has no foundation to critique jihadism. George Weigel, the Distinguished Senior Fellow of Washington's Ethics and Public Policy Center quotes Marcello Pera an agnostic and former president of the Italian Senate, "Europe is infected by an epidemic of relativism. It believes that all cultures are equivalent. It refuses to judge them, thinking that to accept and defend one's own culture would be an act of hegemony, of intolerance, that betrayed an anti-democratic, anti-liberal, disrespectful attitude toward the autonomy of other populations and individuals." [6]

As defined by prominent Christian thinker and catholic priest Richard John Neuhaus: "Jihadism is the religiously inspired ideology (which teaches) that it is the moral obligation of all Muslims to employ whatever means (are) necessary to compel the world's submission to Islam." [7]

This is not saying that all Muslims are jihadists in the same way that not all Christians are successful in demonstrating acts of charity. Further, the history of the Church is not a history that has always demonstrated Christ in ways that revealed Jesus as the hope and the light of the world.

Weigel distinguishes Muslims, as a whole, and jihadism in this way, "Jihadism is distinguished from other forms of Islamism or the ill-named 'Islamic fundamentalism' by its distinctive views on Islamic reform, by its political methods and goals (which are messianic and involve nothing less than a global Islamic state), by its concept of its enemies and by the methods it legitimizes for dealing with these enemies." [8]

Is it any wonder that homicidal/suicidal bombers (homicide is the intent and suicide is one of the many tragic consequences) are occurring throughout the world?

Jihadists are not crazy! They make, to themselves, a terrible kind of sense. [9]

---

6   George Weigel, *Faith, Reason and the War Against Jihadism: A Call to Action* (Doubleday a division of Random House, Inc.: New York, New York) 2007, p. 110

7   Ibid, p. 35-36.

8   Ibid, p. 35.

9   Ibid, p. 58.

Within this worldview only those within the same worldview hold and own truth. The British American historian and thinker Benard Lewis summarizes this point on truth when he writes, "The Islamic state (is) the only legitimate power on earth and the Islamic community the sole repository of truth and enlightenment, surrounded on all sides by an outer darkness of barbarism and unbelief." [10]

It should come as no surprise the desire seen throughout the world in places like Syria, Iraq and Nigeria, to name a few, the violent attempts to create autonomous, self-ruled societies created by any means necessary. The need to exterminate or forcefully remove non-believers would not been understood as an evil but rather it could be celebrated as a "holy endeavor"!

It should be easily understood that relativism and those who hold this worldview would be hated by jihadists since relativism negates any concept of absolute truth. Including an absolute truth known in Allah that the jihadist is willing to live, kill and die for.

There is a consistency and tenacity in this form of thought. After all, someone willing to "blow themselves up" in the hope of killing others and thus bringing to fulfillment a new world order is someone who is *"all in"*!

Weigel ominously predicts that the current phase of violent/terrorist jihadism will last at least two or three generations. [11]

---

10   Ibid, p. 31.
11   Ibid, p. 72.

Understanding a framework for Christianity, relativism and jihadism is a necessary start. In the following chapters we will examine tangible ways the Christian can live into the good news and hope of the gospel of Jesus Christ in a world of differences, despair, conflict, harmony, diversity and love.

True Freedom

For freedom Christ has set us free.
Stand firm, therefore, and do not submit
again to a yoke
of slavery.

Galatians 5:1

Relativism elevates individual liberties, individual thought and individual freedoms. It is therefore odd at first to consider the struggles relativism experiences with spiritual or physical confinement that do not demonstrate freedom. As mentioned earlier relativism struggles with meaning in life. An "anything goes but nothing really matters" worldview does not elevate the spirit. Rather, it begins to wear on and depress the spirit. Ultimately, a person may even begin to consider the value and meaning of life itself. Is it then any wonder that some areas of the world where relativism is firmly a fabric of society that declining birth rates often occur? Why bring a new life into a world that ultimately has no meaning?

Relativism and its "live for today" mantra can also lead to the embracing of destructive lifestyles. At times, this can include various types of addictions. It is safe to say that anyone who is an addict to something would not boast of feeling free! Rather, one is living as a slave to whatever the individual is addicted too,

A jihadist worldview will not understand freedom in the same way as a Christian. Therefore, a homicidal/suicidal attack might be understood as an act of faith by the jihadist and an indication to a slavery to a false teaching for a Christian.

How is the Christian response of good news and hope possible considering the many struggles faced today? First, is the conviction that God is alive and active in the world and in personal lives. God is always up to more than we can know. God is always working through the cross and resurrection of Jesus Christ at more than one angle.

In Paul's letter to the church in Galatia he addresses the issues of freedom and slavery and invites us to broaden our understanding of what we might be a slave to?

Are we a slave to money? Is it fear rooted in personal pain? Revenge? Works? Guilt and cultural rigidity? Power? Climbing the ladder of success?

The Christian message addresses all these and offers true freedom! To the challenge of money and the temptation to live for money and the acquisition of stuff the apostle Paul offers this alternative. *Bear one another's burdens, and in this way, you will fulfill the law of Christ (Galatians 6:2).*

The writer, teacher, speaker and Christian woman Joyce Meyers is someone who knows from personal experience the reality of spiritual and emotional slavery found in fear rooted in personal pain. It is why she is an inspiration to many around the world regardless of their Christian or religious affiliation. She meets people at an emotional level and offers a ray of hope. In her book, *Beauty for Ashes: Receiving Emotional Healing*, she writes, "God is a Champion at bringing people from a place of destruction to a place of total victory. As they reach that place of victory, they become trophies of His grace, and they are set on display as a fragrant reminder of God's goodness. I share my testimony in this book to help those who are still in the process of becoming a trophy for God."[12]

Born in Holland on April 15, 1892 was a woman who rightly understood the call for revenge, however, instead chose grace and forgiveness and new life. Corrie Ten Boom was a Christian woman in the Lutheran tradition. She worked with her father and sister as watchmakers. In her 50's life would make a dramatic change as the Nazi's rose to power and would over-run Holland. Soon the plight of the Jews would become a living reality and she like many others within her community would have to make decisions of conscience and sacrifice. In her book, *The Hiding Place*[13] she tells the story of her life and gives testimony of her faith and her cry for grace and forgiveness, not revenge, to her captors. Those who treated her and those she loved with brutality and death.

The temptation in works (meaning any human action placed in front of God's grace) can take many different forms. And placing human action to earn God's grace (whatever that human action might be) can develop into a type of works. The apostle Paul proclaims to the Galatian church struggling with incorporating Jewish law, food rituals and circumcision into the Christian life of faith with these words, *For in Christ Jesus neither circumcision nor uncircumcision counts for anything; the only thing that counts is faith working through love (Galatians 5:6).*

In John Wesley's day in the 1700's in England the challenge of works was seen in the common persons access to the church and thus the sacraments of the church, specifically, baptism and communion. In his day, many

12   Joyce Meyer, *Beauty for Ashes: Receiving Emotional Healing* (Warner Faith a division of AOL Time Warner Book Group: USA) 2003, p. 4.
13   Corrie Ten Boom, *The Hiding Place* (Barbour Publishing, Inc.: Uhrichsville, Ohio) 1971.

of the common folk struggled with church attendance largely due to cultural norms, education and the societal system that governed everyday life. In this way, the reality was many, if not most people did not attend church and therefore receive the sacraments of communion and baptism. In response to this Wesley decided to go to where the people were and conduct open air preaching of God's good news, followed by an open table invitation to communion. The shocking reality of this gift of free grace was people who weren't even baptized but stirred in the spirit would come forward and receive communion! A scandalous action in his day! Further, there were times when persons would hear the Word preached, be baptized and receive communion all in the same day; with no church membership or education!

In each of these situations, and many others throughout the ages, the Church has learned and re-learned the lesson that while a human action may be a beautiful means of grace. It still remains a means of grace and not a human requirement to then attain or earn God's grace. *Yet we know that a person is justified not by the works of the law but through faith in Jesus Christ. And we have come to believe in Christ Jesus, so that we might be justified by faith in Christ, and not by doing the works of the law; because no one will be justified through the works of the law (Galatians 2:16).*

Jesus and the woman caught in adultery (John 7:53-8:11) informs us on the issues of guilt and cultural rigidity and the freedom and new life known in all these things as a gift from Jesus. *Then each of them went home, while Jesus went to the Mount of Olives. Early in the morning he came again to the temple. All the people came to him and he sat down and began to teach them. The scribes and the Pharisees brought a woman who had been caught in adultery; and making her stand before all of them, they said to him, "Teacher, this woman was caught in the very act of committing adultery. Now in the law Moses commanded us to stone such woman. Now what do you say?" They said this to test him, so that they might have some charge to bring against him. Jesus bent down and wrote with his finger on the ground. When they kept on questioning him, he straightened up and said to them, "Let anyone among you who is without sin be the first to throw a stone at her." And once again he bent down and wrote on the ground. When they heard it, they went away, one by one, beginning with the elders; and Jesus was left alone with the woman standing before him. Jesus straightened up and said to her, "Woman, where are they? Has no one condemned you?" She said, "No one, sir!" And Jesus said, "Neither do I condemn you. Go your way, and from now on do not sin again."*

In Jesus day the cultural norm was stoning, and it would have been understood by the crowd as a just act. Jesus through this encounter frees the crowd of this cultural norm, this cultural rigidity, and offers something new. Further, notice that Jesus forgives the woman and offers the gift of new life without requiring her to do anything. Her value and blessedness were intrinsic and a known reality because she was created by God *(John 1:3)*.

The challenge of power and the Christian response to the slavery of power will be examined in detail in the chapter *Unity with Diversity.*

Finally, the lure of climbing the ladder of "success" (whatever that means). The constant desire to climb that ladder of "success" can lead to its own form of slavery. The apostle Paul speaks at length to this form of slavery because he lived it. He knew firsthand what it meant to be a slave to works; a slave to climbing the ladder of "success", a slave to power. This is why he writes so frequently on the topic of grace and not works and freedom in Christ. *For we are a new creation in Christ. (2 Corinthians 5:17)*

To understand Paul's theology, we need to understand his life and his conversion. For the apostle Paul everything starts with his personal encounter with Jesus. To know Paul, we must learn of this experience. *Acts 9:1-18,* tells us of Paul's conversion and about that amazing and faithful Christian man Ananias. (For God is always up to more than we can know. God through the cross and resurrection of Jesus Christ is working at more than one angle.)

In this light, a Christian response is to seek to live our lives as a witness to the freedom known in the grace of Jesus Christ and the blessings known in the fruits of the Spirit which are *love, joy, peace, patience, kindness, generosity, faithfulness, gentleness and self-control for there is no law against such things (Galatians 5:22).*

Love is a Direction

So let us never grow weary in doing what is
right,
for we will reap at harvest -time, if we do
not give up.

Galatians 6:9

For the past 8+ years working as a hospital chaplain specializing in providing care in the Emergency Department has been extremely challenging. The setting in which I work in is a high-volume Emergency Department located in a large metropolitan area and serves over 80,000 patients annually. As you might expect this experience has meant being a calming caring presence in the midst of every imaginable human experience.

There have been heart attacks, strokes, code blues, respiratory stats, gunshot wounds, stabbings, assaults, car accidents, motorcycle accidents, MTV accidents, drownings, chokings, suicides, early baby loss, fetal demises, silly though serious accidents, falling out of trees, insect wounds, allergic reactions, drug overdoses, aortic dissections and deaths. At times, being near to so much pain and sadness can be tiring.

However, the good news is God is present in each of these situations. God is simply with us. As a hospital chaplain we are often a visible reminder of this truth. And the truth that God is with us really does change everything! It does not take away the shock or the anger or the sadness or the despair or the pain, but it does bring a sense of life, a time to simply breathe and in time the hope of a season of healing.

Reading the news and learning the daily occurrences of violence, random accidents, effects of addictions, crime and terrorism can bring about a sense of fatigue. A sense of wondering if the Christian life really does matter and possibly even a questioning if God has abandoned us.

I would like to begin with the apostle Paul reminding us that, *Love Builds Up (I Corinthians 8:1b)* and a story. A few years ago, I had the opportunity to accompany our youngest on an 8th grade trip with his school to Washington D.C. It was a fun and learning adventure!

One of the most striking things to me was when the buses stopped, and everyone got out to see the Rev. Dr. Martin Luther King Jr. monument. It was dark and the monument was lit up. I was struck by the size of the monument and noticed the energy of two busloads of 8th grade students wondering around the monument. The young people were taking pictures and reading some of the many quotes of Rev. Dr. Martin Luther King Jr. that lined the wall surrounding the monument and were also located on the monument itself.

Imagine the words of a Baptist preacher preserved for future generations in Washington D.C.! For, Rev. Dr. Martin Luther King Jr. is first and foremost a Baptist preacher who became a great Civil Rights leader in the United States and throughout the world.

In his book, *Strength to Love* first published in June 1963, we discover a selection of sermons Rev. King wrote and preached. Rev. King wrote these words concerning the relationship between science and religion in a sermon titled, *A Tough Mind and a Tender Heart*, "Science investigates; religion interprets. Science gives man knowledge and power; religion gives man wisdom which is control. Science deals mainly with facts; religion deals mainly with values. The two are not rivals. They are complimentary. Science keeps religion from sinking into the valley of crippling irrationalism and paralyzing obscurantism. Religion prevents science from falling into the marsh of obsolete materialism and moral nihilism." [14]

Later in the same sermon Rev. King writes concerning the societal struggles of the day, "Violence brings only temporary victories; violence, by creating many more social problems than it solves, never brings permanent peace. I am convinced that if we succumb to the temptation to use violence in our struggle for freedom, unborn generations will be the recipients of a long and desolate night of bitterness, and our chief legacy to them will be a never-ending reign of chaos. A voice, echoing through the corridors of time says to every intemperate Peter, 'Put up the sword.' History's clustered with the wreckage of nations that failed to follow Christ. A third way is open in our quest for freedom, namely, non-violent resistance that combines toughmindedness and tenderheartedness and avoids the complacency and do-nothingness of the softminded and the violence and the bitterness of the hardhearted. My belief is that this method must guide our action in the present crisis in race relations. Through non-violent resistance we shall be able to oppose the unjust system and at the same time love the perpetrators of the system. We must work passionately and unrelenting for the full stature as citizens, but may it never be said, my friends, that to gain it we used inferior methods of

---

14 Martin Luther King, Jr., *Strength to Love* (Pocket Books: New York) 1963, p. 3-4.

falsehood, malice, hate and violence." [15]

In another sermon titled, *How should a Christian View Communism,* Rev. King writes, "In contrast to the ethical relativism of Communism, Christianity sets forth a vision of absolute moral values and affirms that God has placed within the very structure of the universe certain moral principles that are fixed and immutable. The law of love as an imperative is the norm for man's actions. Furthermore, Christianity at its best refuses to love by a philosophy of ends justifies the means. Destructive means cannot bring constructive ends, because the means represent the ideal in the making and the-end-in-progress. Immoral means cannot bring moral ends, for the ends are per-existent in the means." [16]

When I know times of weariness; when I look out at the struggles within our communities and the world and feel tired; I like to remind myself of God's fundamental good news known in the gospel of Jesus Christ. I like for the words of St. Paul, *so let us not grow weary in doing what is right (Galatians 6:9a)* to echo in my ear. I like to recall the giants of the faith like Rev. Dr. Martin Luther King Jr. who modeled the strength to love and walk by faith amid apparent impossible odds.

For, God is always up to more than we can know. God is always working through the cross and resurrection of Jesus Christ at more than one angle

---

15   Ibid, p. 7.
16   Ibid, p. 116.

Widening Circles of Love

In this is love,
not that we loved God but that he loved us
an sent his Son to be the atoning sacrifice
for our sins.

I John 4:10

How do you have joy and hope when looking out at the world?

This question really depends on what you are looking at. Are you looking at where man is and what man is up to or are you looking at where God is and what God is up to?

When looking at where man is and what man is up to it can be depressing, chaotic and scary. The world certainly seems to be in a state of transition in many areas. Famines and meeting people's basic needs remain a continuing challenge. Violence and war continue to spur mass migrations and death. Intolerance and hate speech seem to be increasing as competing groups vie for greater influence and prosperity. Focusing on these realities can be depressing, chaotic and scary.

When looking at God, however, at where God is and what God is up to a different vision begins to emerge. A vision of hope, love in action and joy!

How is this possible? How do you have joy and hope when looking out at the world?

It is easy to learn about what man is up to. Simply,

check the news on your cell phone, read a newspaper or watch cable news on TV. It takes some time and some digging and a desire to see more *(John 1:46b)* to learn what God is up to in the world.

And, I promise you will not be disappointed!

Before looking at today let's briefly look to the past for God's promise is to be with us and history demonstrates time and time again God's faithfulness.

Giovanni Bernardone was born in Italy in 1211, in a little town in Italy into a world of moderate comfort. His father was a prosperous merchant. What happened in this man's life to change his circle of love, his realm of kindness to include lepers and the poor? To extend his message of love to those outside his little town who had grown accustomed, amused and maybe even a little inspired by this man, to new areas where others thought of him as a fool and treated him with reproach. What inspired this man we know as St. Francis of Assisi to extend his circle of love to such a great extent that it inspired the Christian church of his day and throughout the ages to examine itself and to widen our circles of persistent kindness and love?

Florence was a Christian woman born in England; who chose in 1854 to leave her life of comfort to help develop efficient, caring nurses during the Crimean War. What inspired this woman to leave her sheltered life of comfort and travel to a distant land and assist the wounded and the dying; to lend support at a time when filth and limited medical practices was the norm; to change the perception and expectation of an entire profession? How many of us and those throughout the world have benefited from the kindness and professionalism of a registered nurse? What was it that inspired Florence Nightingale to widen her circle of love to include the sick, dying and forgotten?

I was born in 1965 in the United States so let's look within the USA during that time. Consider the growth of Christian schools. What about the amazing growth in Christian radio in the last 20 years so that Christian radio has now entered much of mainstream America!

The Emmaus movement is a spiritual retreat of learning and renewal which began in 1990 and continues to breathe life into local churches and individual pilgrims throughout the world! Kairos prison ministry continues to transform lives. Consider the impact Franklin Graham's Samaritans Purse, Operation Christmas Child Shoe Box ministry has had delivering over 135 million shoeboxes to boys and girls in over 130 countries since 1993.[17] Or, consider the sheer scale and magnitude of United Bible Societies which translate scripture into native languages throughout the world. All told in the year 2004 the Societies distributed 390 million versions of scripture, complete or partial.[18]

Growing up in the 1970's and 80's the Cold War struggle between the Soviet Union and the United States was very real. Who could have imagined that the Soviet Union would be no more, and that Russia would be experiencing Christian growth and revival? This would have been considered as impossible since we were taught that the Soviet Union opposed religion and was an atheistic country.

Consider the amazing growth of Christianity in

---

17 https://www.samaritanpurse.org
18 Philip Jenkins, *The New Faces of Christianity: Believing the Bible in the Global South* (Oxford United Press) 2006, p. 24.

places like Africa[19], Vietnam, South Korea and India[20]; to mention only a few areas of the world where growth and revivalism within Christian communities is simply beyond human understanding and rational thinking.

Who would have known that on August 26, 1910, in an area called Skopje (modern day Macedonia) that a baby girl would be born who would grow up to be a slightly built 5ft woman who would transform the world through her acts of charity, love and devotion to the poor and voiceless of the world? What possible impact might Mother Teresa have on the incredible growth of Christianity in India that is occurring today and has been happening for the past few decades!

The last "official" count of Christians in India was done in 2001 and recorded 2.3% of the population or 25 million Christians.[2121]

Getting an accurate count is extremely difficult do to political and cultural reasons within the country. However, modest estimates say that today 6% of the Indian population is Christian and that its growth is occurring throughout economic, regional and cultural backgrounds! Six percent of the Indian population is over 62 million Christians! And, this figure could be quite low since it

---

19   Thomas C. Oden, *How Africa Shaped the Christian Mind: Redis-covering the African Seedbed of Western Christianity* (IVP Books an imprint of InterVarsity Press, Downers Grove, Illinois) 2007, p. 10.

20   Philip Jenkins, *The Next Christendom: The Coming of Global Christianity* (Oxford University Press) 2007, p. 82-84.

comes from the 2000, *World Christian Encyclopedia.*[22]

God is amazing! And the gospel of faith, hope, persistent kindness and love is alive! People are being drawn to the cross of Christ throughout the world at rates that are almost impossible to count! This is happening today! In our lifetimes!

When I look out at the world and what man is up to, I am not naive. I see great challenges and enormous work to be done in God's vineyard *(Matthew 20:1-16)*. There is always a need for more workers in God's vineyard and there is always more work to be done.

At the same time, when I look out at the world and what God is up to, I can rejoice in joy, hope and love and I can seek to do my part in God's vineyard.

---

21   Ibid, 83.
22   Ibid, 83-84.

Unity within Diversity

In the second chapter of this book, *True Freedom,* we looked at various ways a person can be a slave to something; money, fear rooted in personal pain, revenge, works (meaning any human action placed in front of God's grace), guilt and cultural rigidity, power and climbing the ladder of "success".

In this chapter we will examine the issue of power. Being a slave to power. Power the need or desire to dominate or coerce another into submission.

Oddly, relativism struggles with the issue of power. It is a worldview based on promoting individual liberties, individual thought and individual freedoms. Relativism is therefore, limited to the confines of human thought and imagination. Entry into this worldview means conforming to its worldview. One must be like-minded to "join the club" and those seen as outside the group can be understood as narrow-minded or not very smart or not as "highly evolved". At the same time, when those in the relativistic club are in the position of power then non-entry into this worldview can have serious and negative consequences on one's wealth and societal opportunities.

Jihadism also has a distinct view on power and the use of power. Jihadism is limited by its narrow interpretation of its own history and scripture. The result has then led to a very narrow and violent way of promoting social change.

The Christian worldview is not limited by the confines of human thought and imagination. It also, has a very different view on its history and scripture.

As a result, power is understood very differently. Mystery is embraced. For God is alive and God is free!

This difference occurs so often and is so apparent in Christian scriptures that it can be sometimes over-looked. In truth, the Bible has both paradoxical and dualistic thinking!

Perhaps it is this reality that is one of the great gifts the faith has to offer the broader world community. The ability to hold, embrace and encourage various forms of thought.

Some of us within the human family are more apt to embrace dualistic thinking. Some of us within the human family only know peace within paradoxical thinking. God, whose ways are higher than our ways and who has created each person in a precious and beautiful way, seeks out and speaks to each way of thinking in a manner each unique person can hear and understand.

A few scriptural examples:

Everyone then who hears these words of mine and acts on them will be like a wise man who built his house on rock. The rain fell, the floods came, and the winds blew and beat on the house, but it did not fall, because it was founded on rock. And anyone who hears these words of mine and does not act on them will be like a foolish man who built his house on sand. The rain fell, and the floods came, and the winds blew and beat against that house and it fell – and great was its fall! (Matthew 7:24-25)

Jesus taught this parable at the end of the Sermon on the Mount (chapters 5-7 in the gospel of Matthew). It is a parable that speaks in a dualistic way. Either one builds their spiritual house on solid rock that can endure the hardships of life or one does not build their spiritual house on solid rock.

I John 2:22-23 presents another example of dualistic thought. *Who is the liar but the one who denies that Jesus is the Christ? This is the Antichrist, the one who denies the Father and the Son. No one denies the Son has the Father; everyone who confesses the Son has the Father also. (I John 2:22-23)*

Again, there is an either/or proposition. One either denies the identity of Jesus as Christ or one affirms the identity of Jesus as Christ.

An example of paradoxical thinking would include Paul's teaching in I Corinthians 15:53, *For this perishable body must put on imperishability, and this mortal body must put on immortality.*

Another example: *For God so loved the world that he gave his only Son, so that everyone who believes in him may not perish but have eternal life. Indeed, God did not send the Son into the world to condemn the world, but that the world might be saved through him. (John 3:16-17)*

This is a paradoxical thought where Jesus is understood as a very personal Savior who is also the Savior of the world. The prominent theologian Donald Senior wrote on this paradox, "To reveal God is the heart of Jesus' mission and, for John's Gospel, the key to understanding all that Jesus says and does. Jesus takes 'flesh'-that is, takes on a human nature and a human history-in order that God's consuming love for the world would be visible and comprehensible to the world. Revealing God is not the mere dissemination of information about God. What Jesus reveals is that God will not condemn the world but that God loves the world and intends to save it."[23] Later, Senior writes, "The return to God-not only of the Word but of all humanity-is the final purpose of Jesus' mission in the world."[24]

Paradoxical thinking is everywhere in a Christian worldview. The Holy Trinity is a paradox! Life, death and resurrection is a paradox!

As a result of this unity within diversity of thought (this harmony of dualistic and paradoxical thinking) the Christian worldview has been able to embrace the concept of a pluralistic society. A society, where diversity is understood as an opportunity for unity.

Relativism and Jihadism (to name a few) are worldviews that struggle with pluralism within societies because the thought is not built into the fabric of their thought. Because of this it is very difficult to see and then answer the needs of those outside of their own group; it is difficult to recognize the needs and values of those who are not within their own religious or thought worldview.

Do you realize that this is the question "who is my neighbor?" posed to Jesus which leads to the parable of the Good Samaritan *(Luke 10:25-37)* and the realization that there is no one who is NOT my neighbor. For within a Christian worldview everyone is our neighbor!

Further, it is important that the Christian community

---

23   Donald Senior, C.P., *The Passion of Jesus in the Gospel of John* (The Liturgical Press: Collegeville, Minnesota) 1991, p. 16.

24   Ibid, p. 17.

does not shy away from our own history. By maintaining a perspective on our own history, we are able to recall and learn from those moments in history where the church has wandered away from a gospel of love and compassion and peace. We must not neglect of minimize our history. We must learn from it. For we have the witness of the One who is the Good Shepherd *(John 10:11)* and the enduring truth within the Bible to challenge us and prod us to faithfulness when we go astray.

The Catholic theologian George Tavard in his book, *A Way of Love*, writes, "The love that in God, the model of all human love, reminds us that, however important is justice on earth, the ultimate purpose of life is not to establish permanent structures of justice and peace in the world. It is to prepare ourselves for the vision of God and for the total participation in the divine life. To Pilate, who represented oppressive power, Jesus answered: *"My kingdom does not belong to this world" John 18:36).* The kingdom is not ahead of us in humanity's future. It is in God."[25]

With these words Tavard reminds us that our hope, our ultimate hope, does not belong to human structures and powers for all human structures and powers are flawed. Even the church is flawed because it is comprised of flawed human beings. Utopia (regardless of the nobleness of its cause) is never fully acquired in this life. Thus, our ultimate hope must always lay in God.

---

25   George H. Tavard, *A Way of Love* (Orbis Books: Maryknoll, New York) 1977, p. 153-154.

www.ingramcontent.com/pod-product-compliance
Lightning Source LLC
Chambersburg PA
CBHW022045050726
47591CB00003B/956